Did the devil make me do it?

And other questions about Satan,
demons and evil spirits

Mike McKinley

Did the devil make me do it?
And other questions about Satan, demons and evil spirits
Part of the *Questions Christians Ask* series
© Mike McKinley/The Good Book Company, 2013

Published by
The Good Book Company
Tel (UK): 0333 123 0880;
Tel (North America): (1) 866 244 2165
International: +44 (0) 208 942 0880
Email (UK): admin@thegoodbook.co.uk
Email (North America): sales@thegoodbook.com

Websites
UK & Europe: www.thegoodbook.co.uk
North America: www.thegoodbook.com
Australia: www.thegoodbook.com.au
New Zealand: www.thegoodbook.co.nz

Unless otherwise indicated, Scripture quotations are from The Holy Bible, New International Version, NIV Copyright © 1973, 1978, 1984, 2011 by Biblica, Inc. Used by permission. All rights reserved worldwide.

ISBN: 9781908762306

Printed in the UK by CPI Group (UK) Ltd, Croydon, CRO 4YY
Design by André Parker

Contents

Introduction

I have had two conversations with friends that have shaped the way I think about the devil. As a Christian in the United States, Satan played a fairly small role in my understanding of the way the spiritual world worked.

I knew the devil was real and I read about demons in the Bible, but that didn't seem to have much to do with my day-to-day life. In fact, the preachers on the TV who were always going on and on about demons seemed to be slightly insane, obviously deceptive or entirely too interested in the subject for their own mental wellbeing (or quite possibly all three).

Normal people didn't really spend a lot of time thinking about the devil or demons.

Then one summer I remember a friend of mine coming back from a ministry trip to a Caribbean island. He had been there working with a church group, and when he returned he took me to a coffee shop to share what he had experienced.

In hushed tones he described things that he had seen that he could not explain: inanimate objects flying across rooms, strange lights without an obvious source, people standing on rooftops crying out in loud voices, others being healed violently after prayers for their deliverance from evil spirits.

I knew my friend was cynical about these kinds of things, but he was also the most ruthlessly honest person I know. He had concluded that the town he had been visiting was over-run by demons. How could I make room in my mind for a world where these kinds of demonic activities really happened?

Disbelief

Years later, another good friend returned from living in a major African city. He had been studying at a seminary in that country and told me how all the Christians and pastors there spoke about dealing with evil spirits as if they were a normal part of Christian ministry. Their duties as pastors required them to interact regularly with people that were under the influence and attack of demons.

When my friend mentioned to his classmates that most Americans don't believe in the devil (a 2009 poll of American Christians revealed that 60% of them didn't believe that the devil was real), they could not stop laughing at the ignorance of westerners. It was roughly like saying to them that most Americans don't believe in cheese or anxiety or the month of July; it was just denying an inescapable reality of life.

I struggled to figure out why these experiences seemed

to be so foreign to my experience of life. It seemed as if the old C.S. Lewis line from *The Screwtape Letters* might be right after all:

There are two equal and opposite errors into which our race can fall about the devils. One is to disbelieve in their existence. The other is to believe, and to feel an excessive and unhealthy interest in them. They themselves are equally pleased by both errors, and hail a materialist or magician with the same delight.

If my friends and their experiences were correct and demonic realities were in fact a normal part of life here on earth, then I was surely walking around unaware of some important facts about the world I lived in! Perhaps Satan's greatest trick is getting billions of people to forget that he exists.

But, startling as that was, I never knew exactly what to do with this information. Did it matter that I wasn't aware of evil spirits in my day-to-day walk with God? Should I start looking for the devil underneath my struggles with sin and behind the otherwise normal aspects of my life? Or should I just press on living my life—trusting that God would take care of the details? Could I be falling victim to the devil just by not being aware of him?

After I became a pastor, I learned that a lot of the people in my congregation were asking these same questions. Maybe you are as well.

Well, it is my hope that this book can help to answer

some of the questions you may have about the devil and evil spirits. But before we get started, let me just put all of my cards on the table so that you know where I am coming from...

I believe that the Bible is true. We must believe what it tells us and live accordingly. Logic, feelings, and personal experiences may make some valuable contributions to understanding this subject, but they are secondary and subservient to the word of God.

I also believe that the Bible *doesn't tell us everything we might like to know about the devil.* We should not expect that all of our curiosity will be satisfied and all of our questions will be answered. But it is enough that God has told us what we need to know.

The Bible is always true, *but some passages are clearer and easier to understand than others.* There will be times when we must be humble enough to leave it at: "This seems to be the teaching of Scripture, but it is not explicit". It is not normally wise to speculate when dealing with a subject that inspires this much imagination and superstition.

Whenever possible, I have tried to show how I have reached my conclusions from the Bible. I encourage you to read on with an open Bible nearby so that you can carefully examine what it says for yourself.

We should always study God's word with a commitment to humility, prayers for understanding, and an intention to obey.

Let's get started by asking some basic questions about who Satan is and what he does...

Chapter 1

Origins: Where did Satan come from?

If you start reading the Bible on page one, everything seems to go just about the way you'd expect. You've got God, the Creator and Designer of an amazing world. You've got the creation itself, which reflects God's genius in its diversity and grandeur. And at the pinnacle of creation you have mankind, made in God's image and charged to rule over creation under God's authority. But somewhere around page three or four (depending on the size of your Bible) you read something that seems utterly out of place:

> Now the serpent was more crafty than any of the wild animals the Lord God had made. He said to the woman, "Did God really say, 'You must not eat from any tree in the garden'? *Genesis 3 v 1*

What!?

Here in God's perfect creation—a world that God made out of nothing, a world that he designed and controls—something has gone rogue. One of God's creatures is now trying to undermine his authority and bring down humankind.

That raises a huge number of questions! And while the Bible doesn't tell us everything we might want to know about the devil, we can be confident that God has told us everything we need to know. So let's take a look at what the Bible tells us about this subject.

Who is the serpent of Genesis 3?

Genesis doesn't explain where the serpent came from or why he was trying to tempt Eve. All we are specifically told is that it was part of God's creation, but it was *craftier* than all the other animals. But it is clear from the beginning that we are dealing with more than your garden-variety snake.

First, it is able to *talk*. I don't know where you live, but in my neck of the woods we don't have a lot of talking animals. And nowhere in Scripture are we led to believe that animals in general had the ability to speak when God first created the world. The only other instance in Scripture of a talking animal is Balaam's donkey (Numbers 22 v 28), and there we are told specifically that "the LORD opened the donkey's mouth". This seems to indicate that the serpent of Genesis 3 was under the control of a personal being.

As the story of the Bible goes on, it becomes clear that this serpent is a manifestation of Satan. The things that the serpent does in the Garden of Eden have the distinct smell of satanic activity. The serpent tempts Eve to disobey God; Satan is referred to as "the tempter" by the authors of the New Testament (Matthew 4 v 3; 1 Thessalonians 3 v 5). The serpent succeeds in deceiving human beings; the Lord Jesus called Satan "the father of lies" (John 8 v 44). And the serpent opposes God's good work; Satan is said to have been "sinning from the beginning" (1 John 3 v 8).

And so it should come as no surprise when John's Revelation makes the connection explicit. In Revelation 12 v 9 we read about the defeat of Satan, and notice how John refers to him:

> The great dragon was hurled down—that ancient serpent called the devil, or Satan, who leads the whole world astray.

In this passage, there is a clear echo of Genesis 3. Satan is the "ancient serpent" who deceives the world. So we can safely conclude that, even though Genesis does not specifically use the name "Satan" in connection with the serpent in the garden, the snake is in fact a manifestation of the evil one.

Where did Satan come from?

Scripture is not concerned to tell us much about Satan's origins. He shows up abruptly in Genesis 3 and his presence is then assumed throughout the Bible.

Piecing together the evidence, it seems that Satan was created as an angel. Paul says that he "disguises himself as an angel of light" (2 Corinthians 11 v 14), and the element of disguise is located not in the fact that he appears to be an angel, but that he appears to be an angel "of light". Even though the Bible does not answer every question that we might have about Satan's origins, we can say a few things with certainty:

■ *God created Satan! Nothing exists that was not made by God. God made the world out of nothing, and so all creatures in heaven, on earth, and under the earth owe their existence to God (Colossians 1 v 16). Satan is no exception.*

■ *God created Satan good! Everything that God created was very good (Genesis 1 v 31) and there is no sin, deception, or evil in God (1 John 1 v 5; James 1 v 13). Therefore, we can conclude that when God created Satan, he created him morally pure.*

■ *Some created angels rebelled against God. Seemingly at some point between Genesis 1 v 31 (where everything is very good) and Genesis 3 v 1 (the serpent in the garden), some angels turned against God and became wicked (their rebellion is spoken of in 2 Peter 2 v 4 and Jude v 6). We'll think more about this in chapter 3.*

■ *Satan has authority in the realm of demons. At several points in the Bible, Satan is spoken of as the leader of the demonic forces (John 12 v 31 and Ephesians 2 v 2). We also see Satan taking leadership in the work of attacking and tempting God's people (Job 1 v 6; 1 Chronicles 21 v 1; Zechariah 3 v 1).*

■ *Satan's evil came from within himself. He was not*

tempted and led astray (for there was no one to tempt him) but he produced sin and deceit from within himself (John 8 v 44).

So Satan is the leader of the pack of angels who rebelled against God, and he was cast out of God's presence.

There is quite a bit of mystery here that we simply cannot know or understand. We do not know how it is that a morally pure creature could rebel against God. We do not know why a group of angels would choose to follow Satan in his rebellion. It seems wise for us to be careful about speculating beyond those basic facts.

What about Isaiah 14 v 12-15?

Many Christians throughout history have understood Isaiah 14 v 12-15 to give an account of Satan's fall from heaven. In that passage we read:

> How you have fallen from heaven, morning star, son of the dawn! You have been cast down to the earth, you who once laid low the nations! You said in your heart, "I will ascend to the heavens; I will raise my throne above the stars of God; I will sit enthroned on the mount of assembly, on the utmost heights of Mount Zaphon. I will ascend above the tops of the clouds; I will make myself like the Most High." But you are brought down to the realm of the dead, to the depths of the pit.

In these verses the prophet describes someone whose heart is consumed by pride and a desire for self-exaltation. This person's ambition deludes them into think-ing that they can be like God, but ultimately they are brought down—they die and are cast into the realm of the dead.

On the face of it that sounds like a pretty convincing back-story for Satan. So much so, in fact, that the name *Lucifer* (from the King James Bible translation of verse 12; the NIV translation for the same word is "morning star") has become a popular name for the devil.

The picture that emerges from this understanding of Isaiah 14 is that Satan (aka *Lucifer*) was once part of God's inner circle—an angel of light, and a glorious part of God's creation. But at some time, and for some reason, he was overcome by his own ambition and tried to make himself at least equal to (if not greater than) God Himself.

This interpretation was popularised through great works of literature such as Chaucer's *Canterbury Tales* and Milton's *Paradise Lost*, both of which seized on Isaiah's vivid imagery and applied it to Satan's fall from grace.

But if you look closely at the context of these verses, it doesn't seem that Isaiah was primarily intending to give us a description of Satan's fall. Chapters 13-23 of Isaiah contain a series of prophecies against the hostile nations surrounding Israel. Chapters 13 – 14 are the first of those prophecies. The verses that are commonly taken to be about Satan (14 v 12-15) come in the mid-dle of this.

But look at how Isaiah himself explains this section of Scripture. In Isaiah 14 v 3-4, we read:

> On the day the Lord gives you relief from your
> suffering and turmoil and from the harsh labour
> forced on you, you will take up this taunt against
> the king of Babylon:

The verses about the fall of the "morning star" come in this section of Isaiah's prophecy. They are part of a song that the people of Israel would sing to taunt the king of Babylon, their long-time oppressor. Though he once shook the world and overthrew its cities (v 16-17), now he has been brought low by God's justice. For all his pomp and power, the king of Babylon is just a frail man like the rest of us (v 10), who will be thrown into his grave and eaten by worms (v 11). You can see how this would be a cause for joy for the people of Israel!

With this context in mind, we can say that it seems very unlikely that in the middle of this larger "taunt song", Isaiah would break (without introduction or explanation) to tell us about Satan's fall. Instead, these words most naturally and clearly apply to the king of Babylon, whose pride and arrogance caused him to forget that he was merely a man.

We may be able to detect something of Satan's activity and motivation lurking behind the king's pride, and perhaps this is why Jesus seems to echo this passage when he talks about Satan's fall in Luke 10 v 18. But we shouldn't understand Isaiah 14 v 12-15 to be an attempt to explain the devil's origins.

Is the devil "real" or just a personification of evil on earth?

For many people in the West, the idea of an evil spirit who plots and plans to oppose God's work seems a bit far-fetched.

Categories like "wicked" and "evil" seem old-fashioned and irrelevant. We tend to use words like "dysfunctional" to describe people's bad behaviour, as if human beings are machines that sometimes do not perform as they should. When people do bad things, we now look to brain chemistry or childhood trauma or larger socio-economic forces for an explanation. There simply doesn't seem to be much room for the devil in a modern world.

In light of this, some Christians wonder if the Bible's teaching about Satan is really just a pre-scientific way of trying to come to grips with and explain the evil that we all experience in the world. Perhaps, when the Bible speaks about Satan, it is just God's way of explaining things in a way that would have made sense to people who believed in evil spirits and demons. But now that we know better, we can find better explanations for why things go wrong here on earth.

It is true that not all evil can be directly attributed to Satan. In fact, if you think about it, the Bible spends relatively little time and energy talking about the activity of demons. Instead, the Bible more normally says that evil springs out of the human heart (Matthew 15 v 19) and flows out in our words (James 3 v 5-6) and our actions (Galatians 5 v 19-21).

We pass on patterns of spiritual depravity to our

children (1 Peter 1 v 18) and in our societal structures (James 4 v 5-6). In short, human beings have proved that they are pretty adept sinners even without direct demonic influence.

But Scripture does say more than that. And in fact, there's no way to make sense of the Bible's teaching if Satan isn't a real and personal being. Look at the different personal activities that are ascribed to the devil:

- *He speaks (Matthew 4 v 6).*

- *He lies (John 8 v 44).*

- *He works (1 John 3 v 8).*

- *He contends (fights) with God's angels (Jude v 9).*

- *He desires (John 8 v 44).*

- *He prowls (1 Peter 5 v 8).*

- *He has designs and plans to outwit believers (2 Corinthians 2 v 11).*

- *He blinds unbelievers (2 Corinthians 4 v 4).*

- *He deceives (Revelation 20 v 2-3).*

- *He has a character (John 8 v 44).*

- *He gets angry (Revelation 12 v 12).*

No impersonal force or generalised concept could be said to do any of these things. These are the behaviours and activities of a *person*. Most convincingly (and importantly!), Jesus Himself at every point treats Satan like a personal being. Jesus called him by name repeatedly, spoke directly to him, and taught about his works and strategies.

The big picture

There is a lot we don't understand about Satan's origins. God doesn't tell us why he allowed the devil to rebel against Him. He doesn't tell us why he didn't destroy Satan a long time ago.

But we must remember that, at the most basic level, he is merely a twisted part of God's creation. He is not a competing god. And as we go on in this book, we will see that he never surprises, out-duels or frustrates God. Satan is still (in the words of Martin Luther) "our ancient foe", but he is not worthy of our fear or anxiety. Jesus has dealt him a death blow (Hebrews 2 v 14); it's now just a matter of waiting for Satan's end to come.

Why does Satan have so many names?

A name tells you a lot about someone, and a bad guy needs an appropriate name. Imagine if Sauron from *The Lord of the Rings* were named "Frank"; it just wouldn't be the same! The Bible uses a lot of different names for the evil one, and each reveals something about his character. Perhaps there are many because he loves to hide and disguise himself...

The devil (Matthew 4 v 1)—Devil is the English version of the Greek word for slanderer.

Satan (1 Chronicles 21 v 1)—Satan is the Hebrew word for "adversary", and at every point in Scripture we see that he is the adversary of God and his people. This name is echoed in 1 Peter 5 v 8, where Peter refers to him as "your enemy the devil".

The tempter (1 Thessalonians 3 v 5)—Satan loves to entice people into sin. Famously, he tried to lure Jesus Himself into sin as well.

The evil one (Matthew 13 v 19)—The devil is the personification of wickedness and the power behind it.

The ruler (or prince) of the power of the air (Ephesians 2 v 2)—Satan exercises spiritual control over his human subjects, referred to later in the verse as the "sons of disobedience".

The prince (or ruler) of this world (John 16 v 11) and **the god of this age (or world)** (2 Corinthians 4 v 4)—The devil's authority is conditional and limited. He only exercises authority in "this world".

Beelzebul (Luke 11 v 15)—This name literally means "lord of the flies". It was originally the name of a false Philistine god, but is used to refer to Satan several times in the New Testament.

Belial (2 Corinthians 6 v 15)—This name means "worthlessness". It shows what the apostle Paul thought of the devil!

The accuser (Revelation 12 v 10)—Satan delights in pressing charges against God's people.

Abbaddon or **Apollyon** (Revelation 9 v 11)—These names means "the one who destroys". Satan creates nothing but seeks to ruin what God has made.

Chapter 2

Activity:
What is Satan like and what does he do?

As I write these words, dusk is setting in outside my office window and there are devils, ghosts, and witches everywhere I look. There are also a lot of Harry Potters, ninjas, Spidermen and, bizarrely, a large lobster. Tonight is Halloween of course, and children in bright costumes are over-running my neighbourhood in search of chocolates that their parents will eat after they have gone to bed.

There are, perhaps, more sinister things going on tonight as well. Christians have been out in our community handing out little brochures that claim to tell *The Truth About Halloween*. According to the leaflet, around the world tonight different spiritual groups celebrate Halloween (or something like it) in honour of the devil, earth spirits, or their ancestors' souls. Tonight is the one of the sacred nights for wiccans, pagans, and devil worshippers. And so what seems like an innocent child-hood ritual is really a gateway to satanic influence.

Which is it?

Is Halloween merely a candy-delivery vehicle for children; an excuse to dress up and have a party? Or is it the night where satanic influences are at their peak, and we must lock our doors and pray for protection?

Well, this isn't a book about Halloween. But it does seem that underlying that debate is a question that is more fundamental: *what is the devil like?*

Is he a joke (with pitchfork, horns, and goatee), a costume for your child to wear? Or is he a sinister and powerful spirit who takes advantage of our naivety? Let's turn now to consider what Scripture tells us about what the devil is like and what he's doing here on earth.

What is Satan trying to accomplish?

At every point in the Bible where Satan is mentioned, he is described as working to undermine and destroy God's creation. God created the angels for his own joy and glory; Satan led a host of angels in rebellion against God. God created humanity to reflect his image and live lives of loving, obedient worship; Satan tempted our first parents to turn against God. He delights in defacing what God has made and opposing what God is doing.

We see in Scripture that when Satan and his demons are at work, they are aiming at a wide range of goals:

■ *Physical suffering: Demons seem to delight in causing pain and physical disability in people (eg: Luke 9 v 39, 42).*

- *Mental and emotional turmoil: Demon-possessed people are often robbed of their ability to behave and think rationally (eg: Mark 5 v 2-5).*

- *False worship: Deuteronomy 32 v 17 identifies the false gods of the people of Canaan as demons. In worshipping them, human beings were in fact bowing down to Satan and his hordes.*

- *Encouraging God's people to sin: From David to Peter, Satan entices God's people to disobey him (eg: 1 Chronicles 21 v 1 and Luke 22 v 31). He schemes against them and opposes them at every point (Ephesians 6 v 10-12).*

- *Preventing God's salvation: In the wilderness, Satan tempted Jesus to abandon God's plan to save his people (Luke 4 v 5-7). When that failed, he tried to get at him through Peter (Mark 8 v 33).*

In short, Satan and his demons are working to undo and prevent all of God's work, if possible. He defaces, though he cannot destroy, the image of God in human beings. He encourages unbelief and wickedness as much as he is able to. He smears filth on the mirror of humanity that should reflect the image of God. In short, he seeks to rob God of the glory that he is due from his creation.

How does Satan work? What are his strategies?
In order to achieve those goals, we see Satan employs certain strategies. It's not always easy to determine a di-

rect satanic influence in a given circumstance, but we can see some broad patterns behind the devil's actions. They include:

- Attack: *In Scripture we see some people who are particularly under the influence and attack of demons. (I prefer those terms to the more common phrase "demon possession"—for reasons we will discuss in the next chapter.) Satan inflicts physical harm and emotional turmoil on these people. He and his demons even attack believers with "flaming arrows" (Ephesians 6 v 16, speaking spiritually rather than literally), seeking to do them spiritual harm.*

- Deception: *Satan is a liar, and lying is his native tongue (John 8 v 44). He deceived Eve (2 Corinthians 11 v 3) and works through false teachers to deceive Christians into believing things that are false about God and about sin (2 Corinthians 11 v 13-15). He blinds unbelievers to the truth about Jesus that would save them (2 Corinthians 4 v 4). In our world, we see Satan's influence in all false religions and worldviews.*

- Temptation: *Satan entices people into sin by playing to their natural frailties, vanity, and sinful cravings (eg: 1 Corinthians 7 v 5 and Acts 5 v 3). In our world we see the finger of the devil behind all kinds of temptations, from pornography to tax evasion.*

- Frustration: *At several places in Scripture, the devil prevented God's servants from accomplishing their plans (eg: 1 Thessalonians 2 v 18). Doubtless Satan still stirs up opposition to Christ and his people and their plans for spreading the gospel whenever he is able to.*

How does Satan relate to God?

One fundamental question that we must address is how the devil and his agenda of hate and destruction exist alongside God and his authority. How is Satan able to operate in these ways in the world? How do God and Satan relate to each other?

Throughout the history of the church, believers have gone off the rails by failing to hold carefully to the teaching of Scripture on these points. Some have erred too far on one side, essentially making Satan into an evil god who is always frustrating the will of the good God. Others have swung over to the other side and emphasised God's control to the point that they functionally make him the author of sin. But while the Bible does not self-consciously answer *every* question we might have on the topic, it does clearly speak to this matter.

If we want to understand the relationship between God and the devil, the place to begin is with this certain fact: *the evil one is always, and in every way, subservient to the will of God.* We see this clearly in the book of Job, where Satan acts on his desire to destroy Job and his faith. This is worth a careful look:

One day the angels came to present themselves before the Lord, and Satan also came with them. The Lord said to Satan, "Where have you come from?"

Satan answered the L<small>ORD</small>, "From roaming through the earth, going back and forth in it."

Then the L<small>ORD</small> said to Satan, "Have you considered my servant Job? There is no-one on earth like him; he is blameless and upright, a man who fears God and shuns evil."

"Does Job fear God for nothing?" Satan replied. "Have you not put a hedge around him and his household and everything he has? You have blessed the work of his hands, so that his flocks and herds are spread throughout the land. But now stretch out your hand and strike everything he has, and he will surely curse you to your face."

The L<small>ORD</small> said to Satan, "Very well, then, everything he has is in your hands, but on the man himself do not lay a finger."

Then Satan went out from the presence of the Lord.

Job 1 v 6-12

Consistent with his nature, Satan (the great accuser), comes before God to cast doubt on Job's loyalty to God. He desires to put Job to the test and afflict him until he rejects the L<small>ORD</small>'s authority in the same way that the devil has.

But notice that Satan can do nothing without the L<small>ORD</small>'s permission. He has no capacity to pursue his agenda apart from the L<small>ORD</small>'s will. God gives Satan the power to test Job by trials, but he does not at first grant him the power to afflict Job's health or life. Only after God gives him permission (Job 2 v 6) can he afflict Job with physical ailments, and even then the devil is not allowed to kill Job. Even though he hates God, Satan cannot defy his authority.

This is seen even more clearly when Jesus began his earthly ministry. Immediately after his baptism and temptation, Jesus demonstrated his authority over Satan by repeatedly rebuking and silencing demonic spirits. The people around him began to bring demon-possessed people to him for deliverance. They marvelled:

> He even gives orders to evil spirits and they
> obey him.
>
> *Mark 1 v 27*

These demons did not want to be obedient to God's Son—they often kicked and tried to negotiate—but they never disputed the fact that they had no choice in the matter.

At one point in Jesus' ministry, his human enemies decided that he must have received his extraordinary power over demons from Beelzebul, the prince of demons. After pointing out that their way of thinking made no sense (why would Satan cast out Satan?), Jesus taught them:

> But if I drive out demons by the Spirit of God, then
> the kingdom of God has come upon you.
>
> Or again, how can anyone enter a strong man's
> house and carry off his possessions unless he first
> ties up the strong man? Then he can rob his house.
>
> *Matthew 12 v 28-29*

Jesus uses a powerful image to explain what was happening.

Satan, like a strong man guarding the wealth in his house, was holding these demon-possessed humans as his personal treasure in excruciating spiritual captivity. There could be no relief for these possessed people unless someone stronger than the devil came to rescue them. Fortunately, that is exactly what Jesus is—and exactly what he came to do. He is the one with both the power and the will to set Satan's captives free. He is more powerful than the evil one, and so he has "tied up" the devil and robbed his house of its captives.

So the big picture shows us that, while Satan is a powerful being with authority in the realm of demons, he never has independence from God or power that begins to rival God's. He is a limited creature; he cannot be present in all places as the Lord is (Job 1 v 7), and he can do nothing unless the Lord allows him to do so. He cannot frustrate God's purposes or prevent anything from coming to pass. He cannot stop the Lord Jesus from destroying his works and casting out his demons, and the Lord restrains him and his demons at this present time (2 Peter 2 v 4). God has prepared eternal fire for the devil (Matthew 25 v 41), and there is a coming day when he will no longer afflict God's people (Revelation 20 v 10).

But hold on... if God is stronger than Satan, how is Satan able to do anything?

It's all well and good to say that the LORD is stronger than Satan. It's certainly good that the devil can do nothing without the LORD's permission. But that raises a lot of difficult questions as well. If the LORD has the power to stop Satan, why doesn't he do it? Why does he allow the devil to do anything? Why not chain him in Hell now? Perhaps turning back to the story of Job will help us see things more clearly.

As Job's story continues, Satan is clearly the agent of his suffering. He leaves the presence of the LORD and orchestrates the death of Job's children and the loss of his property. By the middle of chapter 2, Satan has left Job with nothing but a shrewish wife and sores from his head to his feet.

But something really surprising happens in the next chapters. When Job, his wife and his friends reflect on what has happened to him, they all believe that this suffering *comes directly from the LORD*!

Job's wife encourages him to "curse God and die" (Job 2 v 9). His counsellors assume that these events must be signs of God's displeasure and discipline in response to some sin in his life (eg: Job 5 v 17). Even Job himself understands that these horrible events come from the hand of the LORD. At one point he cries out:

> The arrows of the Almighty are in me, my spirit drinks in their poison; God's terrors are marshalled against me.
> *Job 6 v 4*

Now on the face of it, that doesn't seem right! For those of us who have had a look "behind the scenes" in chapters 1 and 2, we know that Satan is the one who stands behind this mess. And so, when God shows up at the end of the book of Job, we expect that he is going to straighten things out. The reader anticipates that God will say something like: *Don't blame me, Job; this wasn't my doing. Pin this one on the devil.*

But in fact that is *not* what God says at all. In chapters 38 – 42 of this intriguing book, God answers directly to defend his ways to his servant Job, and to everyone present who claims to have understood the reasons for his suffering. And God's defence, stated through a series of questions to Job, boils down to two fundamental points:

First, the Lord shows Job that he lacks the *knowledge* to understand God's ways. He shows Job that he is playing a dangerous game when he presumes to understand all the ways of the Almighty One. The LORD asks him:

> Where were you when I laid the earth's foundation? Tell me, if you understand. Who marked off its dimensions? Surely you know! Who stretched a measuring line across it? On what were its footings set, or who laid its cornerstone—while the morning stars sang together and all the angels shouted for joy? *Job 38 v 4-7*

Second, the Lord shows Job that he does not have the foggiest idea about God's power and might. Again he asks:

> Would you discredit my justice? Would you condemn me to justify yourself? Do you have an arm like God's, and can your voice thunder like his?

Then adorn yourself with glory and splendour, and clothe yourself in honour and majesty.

Job 40 v 8-10

This is crucially important for us to see. When Job questions God's ways, he is really asking the LORD: "Why did You allow Satan to do this to me?" And the Lord answers him—not with apologies or explanations or clarifications—but with the strongest possible assertion of his own sovereignty and wisdom. God basically says: *You cannot possibly know or understand My ways in these matters.*

How could God let Satan do those things to Job? How can God let Satan terrorise our world today? How do I cope when my own life is filled with suffering and pain? As we consider the question that plagued Job, we should respond as Job did when reminded of God's wisdom and sovereignty:

Then Job replied to the LORD: "I know that you can do all things; no plan of yours can be thwarted. You asked, 'Who is this that obscures my counsel without knowledge?' Surely I spoke of things I did not understand, things too wonderful for me to know...

"Therefore I despise myself and repent in dust and ashes." *Job 42 v 1-3, 6*

That might not seem like the most satisfying way to resolve all our questions. We might long for God to give an accounting of all his ways. But ultimately we must be humble and say God knows what is best.

So does God "use" Satan for the benefit of his people?

There is a larger lesson to be learned from the story of Job, however. It is interesting that while God never gives Job a direct answer regarding *why* he allowed Satan to do these things, he does *show* Job something of his larger purposes.

After all the dust settled in Job's life, God restored to him twice as much as he had possessed before his troubles began (Job 42 v 10). The LORD gave him ten children and many possessions to replace what he had lost. Ultimately, Job lived for another 140 years and died a blessed man (Job 42 v 17).

Thousands of years later, James wrote to Christians to encourage them to remain steadfast in the light of suffering that didn't make sense at the time. And James used the example of Job to teach the church something important about God and his ways:

> Brothers and sisters, as an example of patience in the face of suffering, take the prophets who spoke in the name of the Lord. As you know, we count as blessed those who have persevered. You have heard of Job's perseverance and have seen what the Lord finally brought about. The Lord is full of compassion and mercy. *James 5 v 10-11*

Do you see the point James is making? God's decision to allow Satan to afflict Job was part of a bigger plan. In the end, Job not only learned a life-changing (if painful) lesson about God, but also received back more than he ever lost. Despite the appearances, God was using Satan's wicked malice to show his mercy and compassion to Job.

And so it is true that God does use Satan and his schemes to bless his people and accomplish his will. We see this in the crucifixion of Christ, where the treachery and malice of the evil one was used by God to bring about the salvation of God's people.

We see this in the "messenger from Satan" which was used by God to keep the apostle Paul from becoming conceited (2 Corinthians 12 v 7). So while Satan's attacks may be extremely painful for us, and while his schemes are never intended for good, God promises that he will *always* work all things together for the ultimate good of his people (Romans 8 v 28).

And so, the ultimate way for believers to battle against the evil one is to resolve in our hearts and minds that we will trust God's goodness and wisdom in all circumstances.

Chapter 3

Control: What is demon possession?

emons make for great entertainment. From rock-band names to video games to movies, it seems that a lot of people are trying to cash in on our fascination with (and nervousness about) demons.

There is something about the idea of evils spirits that captures the imagination of many people, including Christians. But, for the most part, our common conceptions about demons are more shaped by films (eg: Linda Blair's head spinning around and spewing split-pea soup in *The Exorcist*) than by biblical truth. So let's leave behind the popular culture and myths, and look at what Scripture says.

What are demons?

We have already seen a little bit about demons when we thought about Satan and his origins in chapter one, but let's dig a little deeper. Two passages of the Bible are particularly relevant. In 2 Peter, the apostle speaks about angels who sin:

> God did not spare angels when they sinned, but sent them to hell, putting them in chains of darkness to be held for judgment.   *2 Peter 2 v 4*

And in the book of Jude, we read:

> And the angels who did not keep their positions of authority but abandoned their proper dwelling— these he has kept in darkness, bound with everlasting chains for judgment on the great Day.
>
> *Jude v 6*

So these angels were once in heaven ("their proper dwelling"), but they sinned against God, presumably by some act of rebellion where they kicked against the status they had been created to occupy ("did not keep their positions of authority").

As punishment for their rebellion, all the sinful angels have been sent to hell and are held with chains until judgment day. This cannot mean that demons are unable to move about the world and exercise influence for evil, for we have clear evidence from the New Testament authors that this is not the case. Instead, it seems to mean that demons have been cast out of the blessedness of heaven that they once enjoyed and are now consigned to darkness, ultimate futility, and the certainty of future judgment.

Given the witness of Scripture, it seems clear that these fallen angels are under the authority of Satan (who is himself a fallen angel). When Satan is thrown down to heaven in the book of Revelation, the demons that are thrown down with him are referred to as "his angels" (Revelation 12 v 9).

At one point some of Jesus' enemies refer to the devil as "the prince of demons" (Matthew 9 v 34), though it is not clear whether they got that information from a reliable source. He is referred to as "the ruler of this world" (John 16 v 11) and "the prince of the powers of the air" (Ephesians 2 v 2), which indicates that Satan occupies a position of authority. In addition, Satan appears to have unique access to God, since he is able to accuse Christians before God (Revelation 12 v 10) and even tempt Jesus in the wilderness (Matthew 4 v 1-11).

But while demons clearly have power in the spiritual realm, it is also clear that *they are limited.* They sometimes appear to attack people in groups (eg: Luke 8 v 2), which surely would not be necessary if each individual demon had unlimited power. There are degrees of wickedness in the demonic realm; some demons are worse than others (Matthew 12 v 45). They cannot be in all places at all times as God can, but must come and go like creatures (eg: Luke 12 v 43). They do not know everything, for only God knows the future (Isaiah 46 v 9-10) and is said to know the thoughts of the mind and the intentions of the heart (Revelation 2 v 23 and Hebrews 4 v 12-13).

So what is demon possession?

The Bible speaks of demons participating in a number of different activities. At different times they *oppress people* (Mark 1 v 32), *enter into people* (Luke 8 v 30), *beg for mercy* (Matthew 8 v 31), *speak through human beings* (Mark 1 v 24), and *go out of people* (Luke 8 v 38). The Bible even tells us that demons are also astute students of theology (James 2 v 19)!

One thing the Bible doesn't tell us, however, is that demons possess anyone. In fact, several times in Scripture people are said to *have* demons (eg: Luke 4 v 33), *but demons are never said to have people!* The word "possessed" is an unhelpful translation of the Greek word *"daimonizomai"* (the New Testament was originally written in Greek). That word has the sense of being under the influence of a demon, being "demonised" if you will.

When we use the word "possessed" to describe someone in this condition, it gives the impression that when a person is "demonised", they are completely under the control of the evil spirit and have no choice but to succumb to it. But ultimately, that impression does not square with most of the biblical accounts of people who are said to be *"daimonizomai"*.

Look carefully at people who are described as being afflicted by demons in the New Testament. Only two of them are what we normally think of when we think about being "possessed" by a demon: the man at the synagogue in Capernaum in Luke 4 v 33-36 and Mark 1 v 21-28, and the Gerasene demoniac in Luke 8 v 27-38 (also in Matthew 8 and Mark 5). Both of these men have lost control of their mental faculties and are used by the demons as their mouthpiece.

Others experience physical symptoms as a result of demon attack: a boy with epilepsy (Matthew 17 v 14-21), a man who was unable to speak (Luke 11 v 14), and a man who was both blind and mute (Matthew 12 v 22). There is nothing that indicates that these individuals had had their personalities overwhelmed or had been robbed of their mental faculties. The demon's oppression manifested itself in the physical realm.

Finally, it's instructive to note that, sometimes, demon "possession" manifested itself simply in wicked behaviour. When Satan entered into Judas (Luke 22 v 3-6), the rogue disciple was still able to carry on conversations with religious leaders and execute his plan to betray Jesus. The only indication that Satan was influencing him was the hideous wickedness of his choices and actions. Likewise, Satan "filled" Ananias (Acts 5 v 3), but the only evidence was in his words. In fact, even Jesus (John 8 v 52) and John the Baptist (Luke 7 v 33) were accused of being demon possessed by people who did not like their teaching and lifestyle.

So if you put all this evidence together, "demon possession" is a term that we might do well without. While people in the Bible are said to "have a demon" and demons are said to "enter into people", for the most part this "demonizing" results in attack and influence more than that total personality domination implied by the term "possession". Terms like "demonic attack" and "demonic influence" seem to relate more closely to the Biblical evidence.

Are demons just a way of explaining mental illness?

Some people have understood the Bible's description of demon possession simply as a primitive society's way of understanding mental disorders and addictions. Since they did not have the knowledge or vocabulary to account for diagnoses such as paranoia, bipolar disorder or schizophrenia, they imagined that there were personal spiritual beings behind these problems. Thus, Christians living in modern societies can safely move on from the idea of demonic influence to better explanations of human behaviour and suffering.

That explanation sounds reasonable on the face of it, but a closer look reveals that it just doesn't account for the facts. Certainly, some people who are described in the Bible as "demonized" seem to display symptoms similar to those of mental illness (self-harm, bursts of rage, lack of self-control, an inability to live in society) or physical illness (convulsions, blindness, inability to speak). But two main points prevent us from drawing the conclusion that demon possession was just a 1st-century explanation for physical and mental illness:

First, the authors of Scripture understood the difference between medical diagnoses and demon possession. In Matthew 4 v 24, we read about Jesus:

> News about him spread all over Syria, and people brought to him all who were ill with various diseases, those suffering severe pain, the demon-possessed, those having seizures, and the paralysed; and he healed them.

So Matthew is able to distinguish between people with physical illnesses and diseases on one hand, and those who are possessed by demons on the other. If you stop to think about it, it is fairly insulting to imagine that the authors of Scripture couldn't tell the difference.

Second, when Jesus cast demons out of people, they were relieved of their symptoms. So either Jesus was accidentally healing people of mental illness while thinking he was casting out demons, or in fact these people were being attacked by demonic forces. In the example of the Gerasene demoniac (Luke 8 v 26-33), demons came out of the man and went into a herd of nearby pigs. It's not clear how Jesus could send a vague, non-personal mental illness into pigs.

So it is accurate to say that there is an overlap in Scripture between illness (physical and mental) and demonic attack. Demons were sometimes understood to be the cause of physical suffering or mental anguish. But there was never any sense in which the authors of Scripture were confused about the nature of people's problems. So we should certainly not confuse the two today.

Christians and demons

Can a Christian be possessed by a demon? I have been surprised at how often I hear this question as a pastor, but frankly the answer is not a simple one. If by "demon possession" we mean that someone is so controlled by a demon that they are unable to worship God, obey his commands, and control their behaviour, then the answer is clearly "no". Scripture says plainly that the entrance of God's salvation into a believer's life will prevent that kind of satanic control.

- *Sin will not have dominion over Christians, who have been raised with Jesus. Romans 6 v 14*

- *God dwells in his people and walks among them, and thus there can be no fellowship between God's people and Satan. 2 Corinthians 6 v 15-16*

- *The Spirit of God, who lives in believers, is stronger than the devil. 1 John 4 v 4*

- *Believers are no longer citizens of the domain of darkness but are citizens of Jesus' kingdom. Colossians 1 v 13*

So we must reject the idea that a Christian can be possessed, controlled, or dominated by a demon. Jesus has bound Satan and set God's people free from his dominion (Matthew 12 v 29). There is no way for Satan to exercise that kind of authority and power over someone who has been bought by Jesus' blood.

But, if we leave aside the word "possession" and think instead in terms of demonic "influence" or "attack", then we have a clearer sense of how demons relate to God's people. This is what is reflected in the experience of King David, which we read about in the book of 1 Chronicles:

> Satan rose up against Israel and incited David to take a census of Israel. *1 Chronicles 21 v 1*

We are not told how exactly Satan "incited" David, but it was part of a larger satanic programme of opposing God's people. Unlike Job, who withstood Satan's assaults faithfully, it seems that David succumbed to the temptation due to his pride and military ambition. But at no point do we have any reason to think that David (or anyone else in Israel) was unwittingly under the *control* of Satan or his demons.

In the New Testament, we read that Satan tempted Jesus in the wilderness, and that a messenger from Satan harassed the apostle Paul (2 Corinthian 12 v 7) and frustrated his plans (1 Thessalonians 2 v 18). We are also told that the evil one looks to devour believers like a ravenous lion (1 Peter 5 v 8). He schemes against God's people, engages them in spiritual combat and attacks with fiery darts (Ephesians 6 v 11-16). Demons can tempt, influence, and attack God's people, but to say that they can "possess" a Christian doesn't make sense of the biblical evidence.

So should Christians perform exorcisms?

In the popular imagination, the remedy for demonic activity is exorcism. In the movies, exorcists are usually part Roman Catholic priest and part magician. They have unique and mysterious powers to engage demons in spiritual battle by performing rituals on behalf of an afflicted person, which invariably involve holy water, Latin incantations and crucifixes. In the church, some people teach that all Christians have the power and responsibility to enter into this kind of activity. But what does the Bible say on the topic?

Take at look at the way Scripture describes how Jesus interacted with demons. He:

- *Commanded them to come out (Luke 8 v 29)*

- *Silenced them (Luke 4 v 41)*

- *Gave them permission to go into a herd of pigs (Mark 5 v 13)*

- *Rebuked them (Luke 9 v 42)*

- *Cast (drove) them out (this is the term used most commonly in Scripture—Matthew 8 v 16)*

- *Thwarted their work from a distance (Matthew 15 v 22-28)*

- *Released people from their work (Luke 13 v 16)*

- *Saved people from their influence (Luke 8 v 36)*

- *Healed people from demonic oppression (Luke 6 v 18-19).*

And now see how Jesus' disciples interacted with demons. At different places in Scripture we see that they:

- *Exercised authority over demons in Jesus' name (Luke 9 v 1)*

- *Could not cast some demons out (Mark 9 v 28-29)*

- *Got too excited about their new-found power of demons (Luke 10 v 20).*

This power was not limited to the twelve disciples, but was shared by "the seventy two" (Luke 10 v 17), by Philip the evangelist (Acts 8 v 7), the apostle Paul (Acts 16 v 18), and even some random person who may or may not have been a follower of Jesus (Mark 9 v 38-41).

We will think more thoroughly about the relationship between Satan and believers in chapter 5, but for the moment it should be pointed out that nowhere in Scripture are post-resurrection believers commanded or explicitly encouraged to attempt to cast out demons. Instead Christians are told to:

- *Use spiritual gifts given to the church to discern where demonic spiritual influence may be at work (1 Corinthians 12 v 10)*

- *Exercise faith in God through prayer (Matthew 17 v 20 and Mark 9 v 29)*

- *Resist the devil, thus causing him to flee (James 4 v 7 and 1 Peter 5 v 8-9)*

- *Spiritually arm and protect themselves against the devil's attacks (Ephesians 6 v 10-18).*

What are demonic strongholds?

Throughout history, some Christians have promoted the idea that there are certain places where evil influences are concentrated. People talk about and pray against "territorial spirits" that dominate or influence a particular area. Others speak about spirits that tempt people in particular ways, and to particular sins. What are we to make of these ideas?

In 2 Corinthians 10, the apostle Paul elaborates on the way that Christians enter into combat with the evil spiritual forces. He describes how the church battles against the unseen spiritual forces that underlie and empower the world's rebellion against God. Paul writes:

> For though we live in the world, we do not wage war as the world does. The weapons we fight with are not the weapons of the world. On the contrary, they have divine power to demolish strongholds. We demolish arguments and every pretension that sets itself up against the knowledge of God, and we take captive every thought to make it obedient to Christ.
>
> *2 Corinthians 10 v 3-5*

For Paul, to live in this world was to be immersed in a place that was hostile to Christ, a hostility that shows itself in the realm of thoughts and ideas, arguments and pretensions. The world is characterised by a system of thought that is in rebellion against God. And so, in this passage, Paul describes Christians as being on the offensive against these hostile forces; fighting not with physical weapons like guns and bombs, but with minds enlightened by the divine power of the gospel.

Paul mentions that these spiritual weapons with which Christians fight (presumably things like prayer, God's word, the power of the Holy Spirit, and trust in the Lord) all have the power to "destroy strongholds". In those days, a stronghold was a place where an enemy was firmly entrenched and difficult to uproot. If you were invading a land, you would find that the enemy had set up strongholds in strategic places where they could mount a formidable defence.

And so the apostle Paul describes "arguments" and "pretensions" that serve as this kind of stronghold for God's opponents, giving them succour and strength and protection from the Lord's forces. Although Paul never uses the word "demon" in connection with these "strongholds", we are on safe ground in seeing demonic activity behind these anti-God systems of thought, belief, and behaviour.

So while it is not helpful to see demonic strongholds in every single sin and act of human rebellion (for 1 John 2 v 16 reminds us that much evil originates not in demons but in sinful human cravings and boasting pride), we should see something of these strongholds in the godless philosophies, distorted systems of belief, and false religions that plague the world. Where human beings are engaged deeply in these ways of thinking and believing, the world (and the devil) has a "stronghold". But Paul is clear that the message of the gospel and the truth of God's word have the power to demolish these places where unbelief flourishes.

What is Jesus teaching about in Matthew 12 v 43-45?

Perhaps you have read Jesus' words in Matthew 12 v 43-45 and come away scratching your head. If so, you are not alone! We read there:

> When an impure [evil] spirit comes out of a person, it goes through arid places seeking rest and does not find it. Then it says, "I will return to the house I left." When it arrives, it finds the house unoccupied, swept clean and put in order. Then it goes and takes with it seven other spirits more wicked than itself, and they go in and live there. And the final condition of that person is worse than the first. That is how it will be with this wicked generation.

Because this passage of Scripture is frequently used as a primer about what happens when a demon is cast out of someone, it is worth stopping for a moment to see what Jesus is really teaching. Now, these verses do contain some information about demons that we wouldn't have otherwise:

■ *When they are cast out of a human being, they go through arid places. This seems to be confirmed by the fact that Jesus confronted Satan out in the wilderness region (Luke 4 v 1-2). It isn't clear why this is the case, but often in Scripture proximity to sources of water is a sign of God's blessing (eg: Psalm 1 v 3). So it could be that arid desert places represent places where God's blessings are not known.*

- *The condition of a human soul is compared to a home. When the demon is taking up residence, the "host" is like a house that is occupied by a particularly disorderly guest. When the demon leaves, they are like an empty house that has been swept clean.*

- *When demons are not living in a person, they are not "at rest".*

- *Some demons are more wicked than others.*

While all of those things are true, Jesus' main point in this teaching was not to provide us with a guide to demonic behaviour. Instead, in the larger context of Matthew 12, he was making a point about the Pharisees.

In the previous verses (Matthew 12 v 38-42), Jesus taught that both the men of Nineveh and the Queen of Sheba would rise up and condemn that current generation. The idea was that the experience of God's truth and beauty that these Old Testament people had received (through, respectively, Jonah and Solomon) was incredibly small compared to that of the Pharisees and Scribes who had come into direct contact with the Son of God Himself. If the Ninevites and the Sheban Queen responded to God on the basis of such scant evidence, how great would be the condemnation of those who saw Jesus and yet still rejected God (note the very end of verse 45).

It is this warning that Jesus illustrates with his description of demonic activity. He assumes that his hearers already understand the things he is telling them about demons—or at least won't be so surprised by them that they don't listen to the rest of his words. He then uses these details to help us understand a more important theological point. We could sum it up this way: *it is worse to have an experience with God's salvation in Christ but not ultimately embrace it, than never to have that experience at all.*

The person who had the demon cast out was actually better off before he was set free from his oppression! Because he didn't respond properly to Jesus—there's something significant about the fact that the house is unoccupied when the demon returns!—he is now in a *far worse condition*. In the same way, the scribes and Pharisees (and we!) should be on guard lest we neglect God's salvation in Christ.

On the whole, it is probably not in keeping with Jesus' intention for us to turn this passage into a guide for dealing with demonic activity and post-exorcism soul care. Jesus doesn't explain what he means by the idea of our house being "swept clean" or "unoccupied", so we can't confidently say what he means without falling into baseless speculation.

Pulling it all together

Christians need to be careful and wise as they consider the Bible's teaching regarding demons. On one hand, we should not be oblivious to the reality of spiritual forces that seek to attack, tempt, and wound us.

We should pray vigorously against demonic influence in our homes, our families, and our churches. We should resist the devil and vigorously oppose the thought systems and cultural vehicles that he uses to further his wicked agenda.

But this doesn't mean that we should see a devil under every rock. Surely one of Satan's strategies for weakening and distracting Christians is to get us to obsess over him to the point that we lose our perspective and focus.

The Bible does not take the position of giving every malady and problem its own demon—as if there were a demon of post-pizza indigestion, or an evil spirit of defensive ineptitude that keeps the Philadelphia Eagles from winning the Super Bowl every year. Sometimes, the problem is simply you! You just ate too much. The Eagles' linebackers can't tackle.

And so the Bible's instructions to people caught in sin are not to rebuke a demon, but to flee from temptation, confess your sins to one another, and refrain from those sinful behaviours.

What is "spiritual warfare"?

The Bible teaches that the world is, in part, an arena for conflict between powerful spiritual forces. God wages war against Satan in which he enlists and equips angels and his people. Satan and his fallen angels, in return, are waging a war against God, his angels, and his people. The apostle Paul describes this spiritual battle in 2 Corinthians 10 v 3-4:

> For though we live in the world, we do not wage war as the world does. The weapons we fight with are not the weapons of the world.

And again, in Ephesians 6 v 12, Paul speaks about the universal struggle in which believers are engaged:

> For our struggle is not against flesh and blood, but against the rulers, against the authorities, against the powers of this dark world and against the spiritual forces of evil in the heavenly realms.

Behind the seemingly normal day-to-day life of the universe is a cosmic struggle between good and evil. As a result, believers are encouraged to be aware of this warfare, to prepare themselves for it at all times, and to avail themselves of the resources and protection that God has made available to them (Ephesians 6 v 10-18).

Normally, Christian participation in this battle will not seem extraordinary or spectacular (casting out demons, etc). Instead, Scripture tells us that we fight against Satan in the power of the Holy Spirit through means that might seem pretty unspectacular: obedience, prayer, faith, confession, and allowing God's word to shape our thinking.

The spiritual war in which we are engaged is real and dangerous, but it is not an equal contest. Although Satan is a powerful adversary, we must never imagine that this is somehow a conflict between two rival powers or two perfectly matched opponents.

The outcome of this war has already been decided; God is the victor and the devil's destruction has been sealed (Revelation 12 v 12).

Chapter 4

End: How did Jesus defeat Satan?

When Satan and Jesus faced off in the wilderness, the devil desperately tried to get the Son of God to abandon his saving mission. Jesus had taken on human flesh in order to give his life as a ransom for many (Mark 10 v 45), and the Evil One knew that Jesus' sacrifice would be his own final defeat. And so from the very beginning, the devil was hell-bent on preventing the cross. He had tried to have the baby Jesus killed through the wickedness of Herod (Matthew 2 v 16-17), but to no avail. And then in the wilderness, he attempted to derail Jesus' plan. Think for a moment about the three temptations that Satan threw at the Lord:

■ *"If you are the Son of God, command this stone to become bread" (Luke 4 v 3). The tempter was encouraging Jesus to use his power and status for his own comfort and ease rather than sacrifice and service.*

■ *"If you worship me, it will all be yours" (Luke 4 v 7). Jesus was promised a kingdom and authority, but it would come to him through the suffering of the cross. Satan tempts him to short-circuit the cross and receive the kingdoms of the world without the sacrifice.*

■ *"If you are the Son of God, throw yourself down from here" (Luke 4 v 9). Think of the public spectacle if Jesus had jumped from the temple. Either he would have died gruesomely (much to Satan's delight), or he would have dazzled the crowds of onlookers with his power. If Jesus had pulled off a stunt like that, the crowds surely would have hailed him as God's anointed one. And rightly so. But Jesus was meant to receive the praise and adoration of the world by virtue of his sacrifice (Philippians 2 v 8-11; Revelation 5 v 12), not by demonstrations of power.*

These were all very real temptations for the Lord, because they seemed to offer him popularity and "lordship" over people—but without the horrors of the cross.

After this showdown in the wilderness, you can imagine that Satan was left licking his wounds. He had "thrown the kitchen sink" at God's Son, tempting him to abandon his saving mission for the sake of comfort, power, and glory. And at every point he had been soundly rebuffed; he hadn't made a dent in Jesus' purpose or resolve to die for his people. Later on he tried a different plan, influencing Peter to oppose Jesus' plan to go to the cross (remember Jesus' words to Peter in Mark 8 v 33, "Get behind me Satan!"?); nothing worked.

But Satan was not going away without a fight, and so Luke's Gospel tells us that:

> When the devil had finished all this tempting, he left him until an opportune time.   *Luke 4 v 13*

From that point on in Luke's account of Jesus' life, Satan is pretty much off the stage. It's true that throughout Jesus' earthly ministry we see various demonic forces doing their work of devastation and oppression, but it's not until later that we see the "prince of the powers of the air" back in the foreground of the action.

It seems that at some point, the evil one changed his strategy. If he could not stop Jesus from giving up his life for the sins of his people, perhaps he could at least control the terms on which it happened. And so Satan turned from trying to prevent the cross to suicidally promoting it. In the light of the Father's sovereign plan (Acts 2 v 23) and Jesus' unshakeable commitment to obedience, the devil saw that he had no chance to win the ultimate battle. But if Jesus insisted on going to the cross, Satan would make it as painful, treacherous, and damaging as possible.

So, before Jesus celebrated the Last Supper with his disciples, Luke tells us that Satan "entered" Judas (Luke 22 v 3), prompting him to betray Jesus to his enemies. He sought permission to "sift [the disciples] like wheat" (Luke 22 v 31), trying to destroy their faith so that Jesus' death might be the end of his influence. And can we not hear something of the ancient serpent's malicious, murderous hiss in the taunts of the crowd, the accusations of the council, and the mockery of the guards? The Son of God went to the cross wading against a tsunami of Satan's malicious hatred.

The death of death

But what looked like humiliation, defeat, and disgrace turned out to be the victory of our Lord. What looked like Satan's finest hour proved to be his ultimate undoing; the defeat of the tomb gave way to the glorious victory of the resurrection. Here's how the apostle Paul puts it in Colossians 2 v 13-15:

> When you were dead in your sins and in the uncircumcision of your flesh, God made you alive with Christ. He forgave us all our sins, having cancelled the charge of our legal indebtedness, which stood against us and condemned us; he has taken it away, nailing it to the cross. And having disarmed the powers and authorities, he made a public spectacle of them, triumphing over them by the cross.

Now, after reading three quarters of a book about the devil, you're in a good position to see how this is *really* good news! When Paul talks about "the powers and authorities", he is describing the devil and his host of fallen angels (see Ephesians 6 v 12 for a similar example). At the cross, Jesus secured the decisive victory over the power and terror of the fallen angels that align themselves against God and his people.

Paul is telling us that God has disarmed those forces of evil; he has taken away their weapons and left them incapacitated. Satan, the great slanderer, no longer has the power to bring charges against Christians. His accusations about our sin, while they may be factually accurate, will not stick. God has forgiven us and cancelled all the debt of our sin; all of the paperwork that documented our guilt before God has been nailed to the cross. Because of the cross and resurrection, the devil's greatest threat has been neutralised.

But as great as that truth may be, it's just the beginning. It is one thing to know that your enemy no longer has the power to attack you. It is another thing altogether to know that he has been finally defeated and destroyed. Paul tells us that Christ has made a public spectacle of the powers of evil. The image here comes from a common Roman military practice. In a world with no mass media, the most effective way of demonstrating your victory over another army was to march back into your capital city with your bloodied and bedraggled enemies in chains behind you, forming a humiliated parade to the delight of the citizens of the victorious nation. That's what Jesus has done to Satan and his legions. He has triumphed over them and made a public spectacle of their defeat and shame.

And Paul has told us that Jesus has achieved this victory through surprising means. This victory came "by the cross". At no moment did Jesus appear to be more helpless, more defeated, and more at the mercy of Satan and his forces. But in God's wisdom, the cross became the very thing that undid them. The very thing that seemed like their greatest victory became their ultimate humiliating defeat; they are now reduced to serving as demonstrations of Jesus' triumph. In the terms of the promise given in Genesis 3 v 15, the serpent has bruised Jesus' heel at the cross, but Christ has crushed his head.

Now Christians live in a world where the evil one has been soundly defeated. This means that although believers still struggle with sin, they are no longer enslaved to it. Once we were powerless to stop sinning because we were Satan's captives, but now we are unable to continue unchecked in our sin. Since we are God's adopted children, we cannot help but live out the family resemblance. The apostle John writes in 1 John 3 v 8-10:

> The one who does what is sinful is of the devil, because the devil has been sinning from the begin-

Was Christ's death a ransom payment to Satan?

At several place in Scripture, Jesus' death is spoken of in terms of a ransom. For example, Paul writes:

> For there is one God and one mediator between God and mankind, the man Christ Jesus, who gave himself as a ransom for all people.
> *1 Timothy 2 v 5-6*

Some Christians have concluded from this passage and others like it (eg: Mark 10 v 45; Hebrews 9 v 15) that Jesus' death was a ransom payment made to Satan in order to free us from his kingdom and authority. The idea is that we were all rightly Satan's slaves by virtue of our sin, and so the death of Christ was the ransom payment made to the devil for our release.

That theory sounds good at first, but it doesn't hold

ning. The reason the Son of God appeared was to destroy the devil's work. No-one who is born of God will continue to sin, because God's seed remains in them; they cannot go on sinning, because they have been born of God. This is how we know who the children of God are and who the children of the devil are: Anyone who does not do what is right is not God's child.

And although believers will die, death has no final power over them. Death is the penalty for sin, and in conquering our sin Jesus has conquered death; his people need no longer fear it. In Hebrews 2 v 14-15 we read:

up if you think about it. While Jesus' death was the price paid that we might be freed from the domain of darkness, nowhere in Scripture are we led to believe that the payment for our sins was made to Satan.

In fact, the evil one has no authority to demand a payment from God and no right to demand satisfaction for our sin. And as we have seen, he was initially desperate to prevent Jesus from giving his life as a sacrifice for his people. Satan would have been quite content to keep us as his slaves and subjects.

Instead, what Scripture tells us is that the debt incurred by our sin was a debt *to God*. We owed our Creator our worship, love, and obedience, and when we sinned, it was his justice that had to be satisfied.

The evil one is owed nothing but his own destruction. So Jesus' death does have the effect of ransoming us from the power of Satan, but it was a payment made to satisfy the justice of God.

> Since the children have flesh and blood, he too
> shared in their humanity so that by his death he
> might break the power of him who holds the
> power of death—that is, the devil— and free those
> who all their lives were held in slavery by their fear
> of death.

And believers are no longer subjects of Satan's kingdom, but they are held by God's power. In Acts 26 v 17-18 Jesus told the apostle Paul:

> I am sending you to them to open their eyes and
> turn them from darkness to light, and from the
> power of Satan to God, so that they may receive
> forgiveness of sins and a place among those who
> are sanctified by faith in me.

All of these things are true because of the cross. Jesus died as our substitute and fully absorbed the justice that our sins deserved. When he rose from the dead, he conquered death and secured the hope of resurrection for his people. Now Satan has no guilt with which to accuse Christ's people, no power to command them, no prospects of death with which to terrify them.

But why does Satan still have power?

Or to put it another way: if Jesus' death has defeated Satan, why is he still active in the world? Why is he still so effective in blinding the world and tempting God's people?

Throughout the New Testament we see that our salvation has both a *current reality* and a *future final fulfilment*.

Jesus came to *begin* (theologians love the fancy word "inaugurate") the blessings of salvation for his people; when he comes back he will *finalise* (theologians will tell you "consummate") those blessings. So, for example: *we are already made holy ("sanctified") in Christ* (1 Corinthians 1 v 2), but we are *not yet sinless in our day-to-day lives* (1 John 1 v 8). That won't happen until Christ returns and ushers in the new age.

Christ has borne our sins already, but he will return to bring our salvation to completion (Hebrews 9 v 28).

God's people *already* have rest from uncertainty about their spiritual state, but they have *not yet* entered into the final rest of God that awaits them (Hebrews 4 v 9-11).

While those particular facts aren't exactly relevant to the main subject of this book, seeing the larger pattern in the Bible helps us to understand how it is that Satan can be defeated but still at work in the world.

When Jesus came and brought the kingdom of God, he dealt the decisive blow to Satan. He cast out demons as a sign that the kingdom of God had entered into the world and that the devil was on the run. So Satan is already and at this moment to some extent bound (Matthew 12 v 25-29); this is why he cannot prevent the good news about Jesus from spreading all over the world. His activity in our lives is hemmed in by the power of the Holy Spirit and the reality of our forgiveness before God.

But Satan is not yet *finally* defeated. As we have seen in previous chapters, he blinds the minds of unbelievers, tempts believers to sin, and generally still seeks to spread unbelief, pain, and deceit everywhere that he can.

But Scripture does speak of a coming day when Satan's

destruction will be completed. In Revelation 20 John sees a vision of a future day when the forces of the nations, blinded by Satan and pressed into his service, will be destroyed by God. At that point we read about Satan's ultimate fate:

> And the devil, who deceived them, was thrown into the lake of burning sulphur, where the beast and the false prophet had been thrown. They will be tormented day and night for ever and ever.
>
> *Revelation 20 v 10*

At that point, the victory over Satan that Jesus has secured for us by his death will be finally and completely ours. The devil will no longer be able to tempt us. He will no longer have the power to deceive the people of the world. He will never be able to cripple or kill or distort ever again.

So in conclusion, Satan is still at work but his fate is sealed. He cannot win the war he has been waging against God and his people. He is utterly unable to snatch one of God's people out of his hand. And so Satan rages like a fatally wounded animal, lashing out and trying to do damage with his last moments. He is dangerous, but power and authority is found in the name of Christ; the outcome of this battle is not in doubt. Christians fight against the devil and his lies with the *confidence* that comes from knowing that he is defeated, but also with the *caution* that comes from knowing that a dying predator can inflict a painful wound.

Chapter 5

Walk: How should we live in a world where Satan still prowls?

hat does it look like for a Christian to live in a world inhabited by a devious, murderous arch-demon and his army of fallen angels? How do we seek to worship God and enjoy him when an unseen enemy is always working to undermine our efforts?

It sounds a little bit like the plot of a grainy horror movie or the sequel to the *Twilight* series (shudder). But in reality that is exactly the Bible's understanding of life on earth until the Lord Jesus returns. This final chapter explores questions about the place of Satan in Christian spirituality; about how we walk in this world in light of Satan's activity.

We have seen in previous chapters that our Christian lives need to be shaped less by a "spectacular" view of the devil's current work, and more by a sober sense of who Satan is, and what he is doing now. We must be alert and vigilant "in order that Satan might not outwit us" (2 Corinthians 2 v 11).

What are the weapons in Satan's arsenal? How does he try to outwit us? The Bible suggests a few different diabolical strategies:

Temptation

Satan loves to entice human beings into sin. He cannot make us sin, but he knows the pride and anger and lust and anxiety to which we are particularly prone; and he can orchestrate situations where we are most likely to give in. Satan has some authority in this world's system, and so he is able to bring about temptations that incite our passions and stir up our unbelief.

This is why Ephesians 6 v 11 tells us that Christians should be prepared for the "schemes of the devil". Satan is fundamentally a schemer and a plotter; he cannot make his plans and temptations obvious or else he would risk exposure. If people saw the devil and his temptations and traps clearly, they would not walk into them.

Think for a second what it would be like if Satan were to tell the truth when he tempted people? Could you picture what that would look like? Imagine if Satan tried to tempt us honestly; it might go something like this:

Satan: You should cheat on your wife with that good-looking girl in the office.

Person: I don't think so. It's wrong and it would hurt my wife.

Satan: Fair enough; you make a good point. But look, I've run a cost-benefit analysis for you. Here's what I've come up with:

Benefits	Costs
1. A few moments of physical (if perhaps awkward) pleasure.	1. Disobedience to God
	2. Erode your communion with God
	3. Ruin, or possibly even end your marriage
	4. Humiliate your wife
	5. Mess up your kids' lives
	6. Public humiliation and exposure
	7. Might cost you your job
	8. Might mess up your co-worker's life
	9. Diseases?
	10. Unwanted pregnancy?
	11. Dishonour and disgrace on your church
	12. Wreck your witness to others

Person: Yeah, wow. Ummm... no, thanks.

Of course Satan can't tell the truth when he tempts us! If he did, no one in their right mind would fall into his temptations. And so he must deceive and ensnare; he has to masquerade as an angel of light (2 Corinthians 11 v 14). He has to promise that sin can bring us meaning and pleasure and joy that God cannot. He has to try to convince us to value the fleeting pleasures of sin over communion with God. It is a ludicrous strategy, but it works so often.

This is surely part of what the Bible means when it calls us to be "sober-minded" (1 Peter 5 v 8); to weigh up the realities of a situation, rather than be carried away with impressions.

Deceit

Satan thrives on deceit. Like an artist working with clay or oil paints, Satan works with lies. This is why Jesus said of him:

> There is no truth in him. When he lies, he speaks his native language, for he is a liar and the father of lies. *John 8 v 44*

The devil stands behind every false religion and its false way of salvation. He is the inspiration for every false teacher who teaches demonic doctrines in the name of Christ. Every one who teaches lies has the aroma of the evil one around him (1 John 4 v 1-6). He enslaves people in systems of deception and false belief that keep them from loving and knowing the one true God.

And so one of Satan's primary goals is to maximise suffering by convincing human beings to believe things that are not true. Think of all of the lies that have been deeply rooted in human societies. Over the course of history, people have believed that some races are better than others, that men are superior to women, that the rich can exploit the poor whenever they want to. Satan has deceived nations full of people into believing that a devoted widow should throw herself on her husband's funeral pyre, that girl babies should be exposed and left to die, that children should form the labour force for sweat shops. All of these things seem obviously wicked to us, but only because God has mercifully opened our eyes to those evils; you can be sure that our society has its own diabolical blind spots.

That's why soaking ourselves in God's word is so vital for believers. It's only as the Holy Spirit enables us to view the world, the society we live in, our church and ourselves as God sees us that we will become aware of the way we are falling for the devil's deceits.

It's why the strongest means of defending ourselves from the evil one is to give ourselves to meditating on God's word day by day—by regularly meeting with other Christians and hearing God's word preached together; by encouraging each other and "speaking God's word" into each other's lives.

Attack

The apostle Peter warns us that the devil prowls around like a lion, looking for someone to devour (1 Peter 5 v 8). In the context of the letter, which is largely about how Christians should endure times of persecution and suffering, it seems that one of the ways that Satan attacks like a ferocious predator is by bringing suffering into the life of a believer. He aims to shake a believer's trust in God through painful circumstances (think of Job), so that their confidence will be replaced with despair and hopelessness.

This is a formidable weapon, and wherever we see it at work we can be confident that demonic influence is present. But there are limits on the devil's ability to influence believers (thank God!). He may rule in the hearts of unbelievers, but not in the hearts of God's children (1 John 3 v 10). In fact, Scripture tells us that Satan:

- *Cannot undo our salvation. Scripture tells us that God knows those who are his own, and Satan does not have the strength to pluck God's sheep out of his care (John 10 v 28-29).*

- *Cannot force us to do anything. We were once under Satan's power, but we have now turned to God (Acts 26 v 18). We were once dead in our trespasses and sins, unable to do anything but follow Satan. But God has made us alive with Christ and has seated us in the heavenly places (Ephesians 2 v 1-10). Satan can tempt and attack and try to influence us, but he has no final power or authority.*

- *Cannot read our minds. Scripture does not explicitly state that Satan cannot read our minds, but it seems like a safe inference. The Bible describes God over and over again as the One who knows all things (eg: Psalm 139, Isaiah 40 v 28). The Lord Jesus demonstrated his divinity by the fact that he knew the thoughts of men (Matthew 9 v 4). Satan, however, is merely a creature. He does not possess all knowledge and so we can be confident that while he is an astute observer of human behaviour, and may well be able to anticipate what we might think or do in a certain situation, he does not have God-like access to our hearts and minds.*

How do I resist the devil in my day-to-day life?

While we live as believers awaiting the return of Christ and the end of the devil's terrors, we must be careful. If the devil is pacing about like a lion looking for someone to crush and eat, then we should be wide awake and ready for his schemes.

On the night of Jesus' betrayal, the Lord told Peter that Satan wanted to "sift him like wheat" (Luke 22 v 31). In the Garden of Gethsemane, Jesus warned him again to stay awake and pray against the coming temptation (Matthew 26 v 41). Peter slept instead and was ultimately not prepared when Satan attacked.

And so it is no coincidence that when Peter later wrote about resisting the devil, he said that Christians should be "sober-minded" and "watchful" (1 Peter 5 v 8, ESV). We battle against Satan by paying attention; by having a good sense of what he wants and how he works. We should not be ignorant of Satan and his ways, but we should see his trap and snares coming. When sinful temptations come across our path, or when unhelpful thoughts seem to come unbidden from our minds and hearts, we must be able to identify the devil's influence so that we don't give in to them.

Too many Christians feel that they are at the mercy

of the devil and his schemes; that his power is so great that we cannot hope to overcome him in this life. But speaking of the devil, Scripture tells us to "resist him, standing firm in the faith"(1 Peter 5 v 9). The sense is that if we are rooted and firmly balanced on the rock of God's truth, Satan will not be able to move us. And then James makes a wonderful promise: that if we resist the devil, he will flee from us (James 4 v 7).

The apostle Paul gives us a powerful metaphor for this dynamic in Ephesians 6. He compares our preparation for the devil's attacks to a soldier putting on armour before a battle. We read in Ephesians 6 v 10-18:

> Finally, be strong in the Lord and in his mighty power. Put on the full armour of God, so that you can take your stand against the devil's schemes. For our struggle is not against flesh and blood, but against the rulers, against the authorities, against the powers of this dark world and against the spiritual forces of evil in the heavenly realms. Therefore put on the full armour of God, so that when the day of evil comes, you may be able to stand your ground, and after you have done everything, to stand.
>
> Stand firm then, with the belt of truth buckled round your waist, with the breastplate of righteousness in place, and with your feet fitted with the readiness that comes from the gospel of peace. In addition to all this, take up the shield of faith, with which you can extinguish all the flaming arrows of the evil one. Take the helmet of salvation

and the sword of the Spirit, which is the word of God. And pray in the Spirit on all occasions with all kinds of prayers and requests. With this in mind, be alert and always keep on praying for all the Lord's people.

Here Paul is telling us how to fight against Satan. And Paul's advice breaks down into two categories of exhortation. On one hand, he is telling us *in what manner* we should engage Satan. Paul tells Christians to "be strong", "be alert", and "keep on". In the course of just a few verses he commands them to "take your stand", "stand your ground", "stand", and "stand firm".

It's clear that Paul doesn't think that believers should live in terror, quaking at the thought of the devil's assaults. This isn't a time for timidity or laziness; though in the time of temptation, running out of the room might be in order (see Genesis 39 v 11-12)! Spiritual combat calls for strength, persistence, and a steadfast refusal to be moved from God's truth.

On the other hand, Paul is also telling us *with what resources* we fight against Satan's devices. Since our "struggle is not against flesh and blood", the weapons that we use in combat are not the same ones that would be used to fight a war against a human enemy (also see 2 Corinthians 10 v 3-5). If Satan is a liar, we must have God's word at the ready (think of Jesus' answers to the devil in the desert temptation). We must have faith that cannot be convinced of anything that is not true. If Satan hates seeing sinners saved by God's mercy, we must combat him with feet ready to spread the gospel, and

What should I do if I encounter something that looks like demonic activity?

Scenes from Hollywood movies may conjure up images of epic battles between specially trained exorcists representing God, and split-pea-soup-spewing demoniacs, but reality is usually much different.

People who claim to have seen or experienced demonic activity describe everything from supernatural activities (inanimate objects flying across a room) to strange voices to physical sensations to an intense personal sense that evil is present. But what should you do if you suspect that there is demonic activity around you?

First, even though it may be frightening (or at least pretty creepy), *we should not think that this experience is terribly unusual*. In the New Testament we see different kinds of people encountering demonic forces. At different points the Lord Jesus, the twelve apostles, the seventy, and even some non-apostles all engage in direct conflict with demons. The authors of Scripture seem to think that it's the kind of thing that happens.

Now, the Bible doesn't give us a step-by-step manual for handling these kinds of situations. But here are a few suggestions that may prove helpful:

- *Don't freak out.* Whatever is happening, you are still living in God's universe. You can trust that he is in control of the situation. We don't have a spirit of timidity (2 Timothy 1 v 7).

- *Pray.* Our hope is ultimately in God, so the place to begin is by asking for his help. It may also be hearts confident in our salvation. Through prayer and the power of the Holy Spirit, we can be sure that God's mighty power will sustain us in the battle.

Notice also that Paul is writing these instructions *to a church*. The verbs and pronouns are plural. He is telling the church to stand firm and wage war against each satanic attack together. This will happen as churches hear God's word preached, pursue holiness together, and strengthen their faith through the sacraments and fellowship. So while it is appropriate to apply these in-

useful to ask other Christians to join you in prayer as well.

- *Read Scripture.* The word of God is called "the sword of the Spirit" in Ephesians 6 v 17. It is a deadly weapon when wielded in humble faith. It may be particularly useful to read passages that teach about Christ's victory over the evil one (eg: 1 John 3 v 8).

- *Remember* **that Jesus is the most powerful person in the room.** Since there's no reason to think that demons can read our minds, it may be useful to audibly assert to the demon your faith in Jesus and his power.

Scripture doesn't encourage Christians to go around looking for conflicts with evil spirits. But it *does* teach us to anticipate that such encounters may occur. And so we should be spiritually vigilant, avoiding sins that leave our souls sluggish, and daily renewing our confidence in the Lord's power. If as a follower of Christ we encounter demonic activity, we can trust that the Lord will guide and protect us.

structions to our own individual lives, there is a very real way in which we should normally engage in spiritual warfare together in a local congregation.

So, I just sinned. Did the devil make me do it?

The authors of the New Testament almost never speak about a Christian's sin in terms of demonic influence. Paul refers to false teachers that have been captured by the devil to do his will (2 Timothy 2 v 26) and ill-qualified elders in a church are in danger of falling into a snare of the devil (1 Timothy 3 v 6-7), but when he speaks to believers about their sin it is usually in direct terms. So, for example, in Ephesians 4 v 25-32 Paul instructs us:

> Therefore each of you must put off falsehood and speak truthfully to your neighbour, for we are all members of one body. "In your anger do not sin": Do not let the sun go down while you are still angry, and do not give the devil a foothold. Anyone who has been stealing must steal no longer, but must work, doing something useful with their own hands, that they may have something to share with those in need.
>
> Do not let any unwholesome talk come out of your mouths, but only what is helpful for building others up according to their needs, that it may benefit those who listen. And do not grieve the Holy Spirit of God, with whom you were sealed for the day of redemption. Get rid of all bitterness, rage and anger, brawling and slander, along with

every form of malice. Be kind and compassionate
to one another, forgiving each other, just as in
Christ God forgave you.

Paul does indeed mention the devil in this passage, telling us not to give him an opportunity to tempt us by
clinging to anger and rage. But while our sin might give
Satan an opportunity to advance his agenda through
us, Paul doesn't understand our sin to be fundamentally caused by the devil and his demons. Notice that the
apostle doesn't instruct them to beware of the demon of
falsehood or to be on the look-out for an evil spirit that
might tempt them to unwholesome talk. Paul simply
tells them that these things are inappropriate and that
God's people should have nothing to do with them. Sin
isn't evidence of demonic strongholds in our lives; it is
simply disobedience that is inconsistent with our salvation in Christ. We don't need an advanced degree in
demonology in order to be obedient; we don't need ex-
orcisms or deliverances.

So as a Christian, one of my motivations for avoiding
sin is a desire to keep Satan at bay. He wants me to disgrace myself and Christ by indulging in sin. The devil
desires me to be a selfish husband and an impatient father. He is happiest when I am miserable in my sin. I
don't want those habits and patterns in my life, and so
I resist Satan and his temptations. But he has no power
to coerce me. God promises never to let any temptation
come to me that is beyond my capacity to withstand (1
Corinthians 10 v 13). And so the only person that can
make me do anything is me.

Conclusion

In the introduction we reflected on C.S. Lewis's warning that Satan is happy with either our ignorance or our obsession with him and his ways. It seems that the Bible's approach to the topic cuts right down the middle. On one hand, Satan is a real and dangerous opponent; he prowls about and exerts influence in the world and even in our lives. But on the other hand, Christians are not at his mercy. The salvation Christ purchased has set us free from the devil's tyranny, and so we are no longer slaves to sin and death. Instead, we are under the authority of God's Spirit and bearing his fruit in our lives.

So, should we be aware of the devil? *Yes.*

Should we be alert to his motives and ways of working so that we can avoid him? *Absolutely.*

Should we be obsessed with him, looking for a demon lying behind every sin? *No.*

Should we tremble at his power and rage? *Under no circumstances!*

Satan's power and knowledge are limited; his doom is sure. He's not worthy of our time, obsession, and emotions. Instead we live with both of our eyes fixed firmly on Jesus, who has delivered us from the devil's wrath and given us a sure hope that we will one day be rid of him for ever.

Is C.S. Lewis an accurate guide to the devil?

For many, C.S. Lewis's *The Screwtape Letters* is the one book (other than the Bible!) that most influences their understanding of the devil and how he works.

Lewis's fictional account of letters from an arch-tempter to his junior nephew makes for a wonderful read. Lewis is at his best when he is skewering the subtle, everyday way that people fall under the sway of the devil's temptations. But is the book a reliable guide to the evil one?

The answer is "probably" or "mostly". Lewis is brilliant in his ability to see how false beliefs and foolish behaviours creep into normal life; how people unwittingly follow strategies right out of Satan's playbook. But the book doesn't claim to be a theology textbook, and occasionally Lewis makes a statement that isn't supported from Scripture (or at least requires a lot of nuance).

So, for example, in Letter 5, Screwtape complains that God: "often makes prizes of humans who have given their lives for causes he thinks bad on the monstrously sophistical ground that the humans thought them good and were following the best they knew".

That statement could be true, but on its own it is simply not. The God of the Bible is holy and he doesn't accept our best attempts just because they were well intentioned. It is true that God will make prizes (save and be gracious to) of people who have served in bad causes, but only if they come to Christ in repentance and faith and thus find atonement for their sins.

So on the whole, I'd recommend you read *The Screwtape Letters* and benefit from Lewis's insight into the nature of sin and temptation. Just be discerning about what you are reading.

Other titles in this series

What happens when I die?
by Marcus Nodder

We all have questions about death. Despite the strong assurance the Bible gives us about life beyond the grave, Christians are often troubled by other questions. What will happen on the day of judgement? Will we have bodies in heaven? Will there be rewards? These short, simple books are designed to help Christians understand what God has said about these questions in the scriptures.

Who on earth is the Holy Spirit?
by Tim Chester and Christopher de la Hoyde

Many people find it easy to understand about God and Jesus, but struggle to understand quite how and where the Holy Spirit fits into the picture. Who exactly is he? And how does he work in our lives? These short, simple books are designed to help Christians understand what God has said about these questions and many more in the Bible.

Order from your local Good Book website:
North America: www.thegoodbook.com
UK & Europe: www.thegoodbook.co.uk
Australia: www.thegoodbook.com.au
New Zealand: www.thegoodbook.co.nz

thegoodbook
COMPANY
Opening up the Bible

At The Good Book Company, we are dedicated to helping Christians and local churches grow. We believe that God's growth process always starts with hearing clearly what he has said to us through his timeless word—the Bible.

Ever since we opened our doors in 1991, we have been striving to produce resources that honour God in the way the Bible is used. We have grown to become an international provider of user-friendly resources to the Christian community, with believers of all backgrounds and denominations using our Bible studies, books, evangelistic resources, DVD-based courses and training events.

We want to equip ordinary Christians to live for Christ day by day, and churches to grow in their knowledge of God, their love for one another, and the effectiveness of their outreach.

Call us for a discussion of your needs or visit one of our local websites for more information on the resources and services we provide.

UK & Europe: www.thegoodbook.co.uk
North America: www.thegoodbook.com
Australia: www.thegoodbook.com.au
New Zealand: www.thegoodbook.co.nz

UK & Europe: 0333 123 0880
North America: 866 244 2165
Australia: (02) 6100 4211
New Zealand (+64) 3 343 1990

www.christianityexplored.org

Our partner site is a great place for those exploring the Christian faith, with a clear explanation of the good news, powerful testimonies and answers to difficult questions.

One life. What's it all about?